Paternoster Punchline No. 11
Can We Trust the Gospels?

CAN WE TRUST THE GOSPELS?

Nigel Scotland

Exeter
The Paternoster Press

ISBN 0–85364–249–4

Australia:

Emu Book Agencies Ltd.,
63 Berry Street, Granville, N.S.W. 2142

South Africa:

Oxford University Press,
P.O. Box 1141, Cape Town

British Library Cataloguing in Publication Data

Scotland, Nigel
   Can we trust the Gospels?
   1. Bible. New Testament. Gospels – Evidences, authority, etc.
   I. Title
   226'.01   BS2555.5

Made and printed in Great Britain for
The Paternoster Press Paternoster House
3 Mount Radford Crescent Exeter Devon
by Maslands Ltd., Tiverton Devon.

CONTENTS

1 Why we can Trust the Gospels

Gospel criticism disturbs and upsets many Christians. They feel there is something wanton and irreverrent about subjecting the records of Jesus and his teaching to close examination. But the world we live in is based on discovery and scientific investigation. The Gospels cannot be exempted.

Discovery and Science

The period after 1450, for a century and more was one of unparalleled geographical discovery. Columbus and his followers found a new world on the other side of the Atlantic, and the Portuguese played a similar part in the discovery in the East.

These discoveries revealed new horizons, of which the authorities, both secular and religious, clearly had not taken account, and for which they were unprepared.

The close of the sixteenth century saw the beginnings of a great development in the natural sciences. A new interest in the study of physics and mathematics emerged with the impetus given by men like Galileo Galilei (1564–1642) and Isaac Newton (1642–1727), both of whom, incidentally, had a firm belief in God. This bred a spirit of inquiry and curiosity which before long was not confined to natural science.

Biblical Criticism

Gradually these two aspects (discovery and science) began to lead to criticism and questioning of biblical authority. With the advent of printing the Bible became available to every man and it was thus now possible to explain it without the help of the Church.

At this point in time, biblical criticism did exist, but chiefly in the form of 'Lower Criticism'. This kind of criticism seeks to compare different manuscripts, some of which are small fragments and ancient translations, in order to discover what was originally written. By contrast, the task of 'Higher Criticism' or 'Literary Criticism' is to consider questions concerned with the date, authorship, composition, purpose, meaning, and the religious and historical value of the various books.

Higher Critical study of the Bible first began in earnest in the last half of the eighteenth century and developed with increasing assurance and confidence throughout the nineteenth century. Looking back on this development Prof. R. H. Lightfoot wrote: '... there can be little doubt that the study had its roots in the spirit of inquiry and the revolt against the unquestioning acceptance of established authority, which goes back to the Renaissance'.[1]

Higher Criticism was not content to establish the correct reading of the sacred text; everything possible must be learned about the origin, structure and character of the writings which have been handed down. With the development of higher critical techniques, new insights were postulated. In the Old Testament, for example, many scholars inclined to the view that since the early books (Torah and Pentateuch) contained so many elements of the later Jewish theology such as is found in the writings of the prophets, they must therefore have been written after the prophets. (This is not, of course, to imply that such scholars asserted that there were no earlier patriarchal or Mosaic traditions enshrined in these documents.)

Gospel Criticism

Theories were also postulated about the New Testament. The chief of these was that Mark's Gospel is the earliest of the Gospels, having been used by both St. Matthew and St. Luke. This view was first definitely put forward by Karl Lachmann in 1835. Lachmann simply compared the contents of the first three gospels (synoptics = *sun optic* = seen with a common eye) and came to the conclusion that Matthew and Luke had constructed their Gospels on the basis of Mark since they preserved the Marcan order of the material although of course they expand it. This belief, usually known as the 'Marcan hypothesis', has been confirmed in many other ways.

Most recent scholars have believed that 'Matthew' and 'Luke' are both based, not only on Mark, but on a collection of sayings and stories usually referred to as 'Q'. To these two sources they each added different material which is now found only in each of the two Gospels bearing their names.

The concentration on St. Mark's Gospel had one result of great importance to religion. It gives a much more vivid and precise portrait of our Lord than the other Gospels.

In particular, in Mark's Gospel we can discern the real humanity of Jesus much more clearly.

Related to all this was a growing interest in the historical Jesus. In fact from the nineteenth century to the present day this has been the central focus of Gospel criticism and New Testament studies. Just how much history is to be found in the Gospels? In answer to this question many of the more radical critics assert—very little indeed. Thus we find a New Testament scholar such as Norman Perrin making statements like the following:

> It is no longer self-evident that the historical Jesus is, in fact, the central concern of the Christian faith, and it may no longer be assumed that the major aspect of that faith is to follow the dictates, encouragement and challenges of that Jesus.[2]

Commenting on this statement of Perrin, Paul S. Minear, another New Testament scholar, writes:

> Put more bluntly, I believe that Perrin is saying that neither is it possible to recover Christ's commands nor, were it possible, would the believer be obliged to obey them. Moreover I believe that he is speaking here for the great majority of Biblical scholars.[3]

A similarly sceptical view of the historical reliability of the Gospels is suggested by Ernst Kasemann in his *Essays on New Testament Themes.* He writes: ' . . . there are still pieces of the synoptic tradition which the historian has to acknowledge as authentic if he wishes to remain an historian at all.'[4]

Arguments for the Reliability of the Gospel Record

Such a stance towards the basic reliability of the Gospel records can be disturbing to certain sections of the committed Christian community. But it is important to realise that there are also good reasons for accepting the basic reliability of the Gospel record.

1. Eye-Witnesses

We will be well aware, if we have done any basic Bible reading, that there is no account of the life of Jesus in the letters of Paul. The reason for this is probably that the details of our Lord's biography were common knowledge. Paul says at one point in his letter to the Corinthians that there were 500 witnesses to the resurrection, the greater part of whom were alive at the time of his writing (about AD 53). In other words more than 250 witnesses were alive in the middle 50s.

Numbers of New Testament scholars have argued that the gospel material was created by the early Christian community. To give an example, at times the disciples were persecuted and forcibly removed from the synagogues. It is suggested that to encourage these early persecuted Christians, teachers and leaders (including the Apostles) provided words of encouragement, putting into Jesus' mouth predictions that his followers would be cast out of synagogues but that through this they would find blessing and strength. (See the Sermon on the Mount in Matthew 6 and

Luke 12.) There is also some suggestion of this in John 9 where the parents of the man born blind whom Jesus healed are afraid to testify, lest they should be cast out of the synagogue. All this, it should be noted, is really conjecture. Jesus appears to have run into enough conflict with the Jews to make it very likely that he would himself have uttered warnings about persecution at the hands of the Jews.

If we suppose fabrications by the Christian community of this kind, we are faced with a problem: What about the eye witnesses we have mentioned above? They would undoubtedly have challenged the authenticity of the account. This consideration casts doubt on the assumption, made by radical 'form' critics, that the early church was free to invent new sayings and deeds of Jesus without any limit. By contrast, such a distinguished scholar as the late T. W. Manson contended that the source 'Q' (mentioned above) was from the eye witness Matthew and that Mark contains substantial quantities of material which can be identified as Petrine (that is, based on the preaching of the Apostle Peter).[5]

Related to the question of eye-witness is the likelihood that there were in the primitive church....

2. *Tradition Bearers*

In the prologue to his Gospel, Luke mentions 'ministers of the word', who together with eye witnesses, 'delivered' the material to him and to others. Similarly in his writing about the resurrection in 1 Corinthians 15:3 Paul uses the same word 'deliver' and again in his discourse about the institution of the

Lord's Supper in 1 Corinthians 11:23. Donald Guthrie believes

'... it is highly probable that this special function was not only recognised but was officially controlled. Such a factor can be regarded as only hypothetical, but it has strong probability on its side.'[6]

Guthrie posits these 'tradition-bearers' because

'It is more difficult to imagine that the transmission of the traditions of the life and teaching of our Lord would have been left to chance ...'[7] 'There is also much to be said for the view that the "eyewitnesses and ministers of the word" in Luke 1 were the same group and that this group consisted largely of apostles or apostolic men.'[8]

3. *The Accuracy of Oral Tradition*

All scholars are agreed that there was a period of time immediately following the death and resurrection of Jesus when the details which the Gospels record were for the most part shared and passed on by word of mouth. New Testament scholars often refer to this as the 'oral period'. Exactly when this period ended is not easy to say. It depends when one dates the writing of the Gospels. It is generally assumed that the oral period stretched over about thirty years but there is no reason why written sources may not have been developed at the same time. Some scholars argue that a 'sayings source' was all that would be memorised and not biographical details. Vincent Taylor, however, argues that details of Jesus' life would have been remembered because the sayings would have recalled to mind the situation which evoked them. Also that details of Jesus' life would have been remembered because they must have been used by way of illustration.[9]

Now it need not necessarily be supposed that this oral period was a time in which many different garbled and fabricated versions of the life and ministry of Jesus came into being. Studies have shown oriental memory to have been remarkably retentive. Many Jews knew the whole Pentateuch off by heart and many Greeks could recite the whole Iliad. Teaching in school was done by memory. The careful work of B. Gerhardsson is very important at this point. These facts are documented in his *Memory and Manuscript* (1961).

Gerhardsson's main contention is that rabbinical teachers not only taught traditional material, but taught it in set forms and vocabulary which the pupils were expected to learn by heart. There were various mnemonic devices to help them in their task. Since the earliest Christians were Jews, Gerhardsson envisages that they would have followed the rabbinical practices. He also supposes that our Lord instructed his disciples in the same manner. Certainly we do know for a fact that Jesus taught his disciples liturgical prayers such as the Lord's prayer and that liturgical prayers were a part of his devotional life. W. A. Curtis, in *Jesus Christ the Teacher* (1943), brings out the parallels between the teaching of Jesus and the methods of the Rabbis, but also shows the superiority of Jesus.[10]

Gerhardsson's position probably needs modifying but nevertheless he has made an important point that memorization was a cardinal principle in first century religious education and it is impossible to suppose that no use was made of it in early Christian catechesis. Even if it is taken that our Lord was not a conventional Rabbi (and clearly he was not), it does not automatically follow that he would have refused to make use of any memory techniques. The probability is that Jesus repeated his teaching material many times and in many places.

It has also been argued that the first Christian preachers, the Apostles and their associates, used Old Testament fulfilment passages which they knew well to help them recall the gospel events. It is certainly true that because of their conviction that there was a continuity between the Old and New, the early Christians sought to commit to memory and manuscript incidents which emphasised fulfilment.

Other scholars have suggested that the sources on which the gospels are based were written in Aramaic. Their suggestion seems not improbable, since Aramaic was the language of Palestine in the time of Christ and thus the language he would have used in his teaching. They contend that when these sources or parts of them are translated back into Aramaic there is a distinct poetic ring suggesting that the sources were written in such a way as to facilitate easy learning and repetition. Don Cupitt in his publication *'Who was Jesus?'* gives an example of how an English translation from Aramaic can capture this poetic ring:

'Love your enemies,

Bless those who hate you,
Bless those who curse you,
Pray for those who despitefully use you.'

C. C. Torrey and C. F. Burney in *Poetry of Our Lord* (1925) and *The Aramaic Origin of the Fourth Gospel* (1922) were the main exponents of the Aramaic origins of the Gospels.

Professor Matthew Black of St. Andrews in his *Aramaic Approach to the Gospels and Acts* (1967) has criticised the work of Torrey and Burney, arguing that the sources used by the evangelists rather than the Gospels themselves were written in Aramaic. Black argues that there is sufficient evidence for an aramaic sayings source of Jesus behind the Gospels.

4. The Development of the New Testament Canon

It is easy to forget that the first Christians took care to ensure that only trustworthy accounts of the life and teaching of Jesus should be generally accepted. The written Gospels were definitely accepted at a very early period as authoritative. Even before the writing of the Gospels, the apostles were recognised by the Church as its undisputed leaders. They were a unique group whom, apart from Judas, the Church did not replace with successors. They had been specifically chosen by Christ and were men of repute against whose doctrine Christian leaders and preachers measured their ideas and teaching (see for example Galatians 2:2). The Gospels were accepted for use in the early Christian assemblies both because of this standing of their writers and also because what they contained was known to be in accordance with the teaching of the whole apostolic band. The claims of the four Gospels to authenticity must, therefore, have been beyond dispute at an early point in time. Certainly by the first half of the second century they were so widely esteemed that heretical groups such as the Gnostics had taken them over and had even considered it worth while to produce commentaries on them.

By the end of the second century it is clear from all the evidence available that our four Gospels were accepted, not only as authentic, but also as scripture on the same level as the Old Testament. It is clear from the writings of Irenaeus in the middle and late second century that he recognised our four Gospels. Clement of Alexandria cites from other gospels, as, for example from the *Gospel according to the Egyptians,* but he carefully distinguishes them from the four canonical Gospels.

In fact, Dr. Guthrie writes: 'The probability is that from the time of writing the Gospels were so regarded. There is no evidence that the authority of the four Gospels was challenged (except in the case of the Fourth Gospel which was rejected by a small group known as the alogoi).'

It is apparent that when the Church finally came to draw up the New Testament canon it selected for inclusion only those books which were known to have apostolic authority. Matthew and John were apostles in their own right, Mark is generally taken to have written down accurately his accounts from Peter's dictation, whilst Luke was not himself a member of the immediate circle of our Lord's followers but nevertheless a careful writer who worked from apostolic sources as he tells us in his prologue to Luke/Acts. As an example of early tradition as to the apostolic authorship of the Gospels, we may cite Eusebius in his *Ecclesiastical History:*

> Mark, indeed, since he was the interpreter of Peter wrote accurately, but not in order, the things either said or done by the Lord as much as he remembered. For he neither heard the Lord nor followed Him, but afterwards as I have said, (heard and followed) Peter, who fitted his discourses to the needs (of his hearers) but not as if making a narrative of the Lord's sayings; consequently Mark, writing some things as he remembered, erred in nothing; for he was careful of one thing – not to omit anything of the things he had heard or to falsify anything in them.[12]

Guthrie has shown that traditions of this kind must be assumed to be correct, or at least based partially on fact, unless the internal evidence of the Gospel requires otherwise.

5. Archaeology

Recent work in the field of archaeology in particular has shown the Gospels to be historically reliable. At the very least, it can certainly be asserted that no archaeological discovery has cast any doubt on the truth of biblical narrative. Two brief instances may help to illustrate this aspect. John's description of the pool of Bethesda with its five porches was held to be very fanciful and no more than a fabrication to enhance his story. However, in the early 1930s the whole site was unearthed and excavated and found to be exactly as John had described it — complete with the five porches![13] Furthermore, an inscription discovered at the sight also stated the water to have healing properties. Again John's Gospel was held to be of very late date, perhaps A.D. 150 or even later. This meant that John the Apostle and beloved disciple clearly could not have been the author. This late dating of the Fourth Gospel was argued largely on the basis of its emphases on light and darkness which were supposed to be gnostic and taken to show the influence of later gnostic writings of the second century A.D. Then in 1947 a large number of scrolls were discovered at Qumran to the north-west of the Dead Sea. These all belonged to a Jewish community which resided in that vicinity from about 153 B.C. until the war with Rome of A.D. 66–73. Besides many commentaries on the Old Testament, archaeologists unearthed a War Scroll which gives a dramatic description of a battle between the children of Light and the children of Darkness! No longer was it necessary to suppose that John's Gospel must be of late date on the grounds of its light and darkness motifs.

Recent studies, particularly of Luke's Gospel, have demonstrated that Luke was an accurate historian — accurate in the titles he uses and in the dates which occur in his narrative. If Luke is accurate in these facts, we have every reason to suppose a similar degree of accuracy in the other aspects of his account. Seventy years ago, Sir William Ramsay, a famous early historian wrote:

Luke is a historian of the first rank; not merely are his statements of fact trustworthy; he is possessed of the true historic sense; he seizes the important and critical events and shows their true nature at greater length, while he touches lightly or omits much that was valueless for his purpose. In short, this author should be placed with the very greatest of historians.[14]

To-day, Luke's accuracy is still accepted. In his *Luke Historian and Theologian* I. H. Marshall writes:

'On matters of Hellenistic geography and politics, Roman Law and Provincial administration, Luke can be demonstrated to be for the most part a reliable guide.[15]

In Maurice Jones's *The New Testament in the Twentieth Century* (1924) pp 227f there is a skilful summary of the research results that prove the historical trustworthiness of Luke. The more recent booklet of F. F. Bruce, *Are the New Testament Documents Reliable?* also gives a valuable summary of these facts.

6. References outside the New Testament

There is also to be considered the extra-biblical testimony to certain basic facts about Jesus. There is mention of Jesus in Tacitus' *Annals* 15:44, Suetonius' *The Lives of the Caesars*, Nero XVI, Lucian's *The Passing of Peregrinus* 12:13, Josephus, *Antiquities* XVIII, iii, 3 and also in Pliny's letter to the Emperor Trajan. Significantly, all of these are non-Christian writers. Although these references provide only scant information about the birth, ministry, death and resurrection of Jesus, taken as a whole they establish the existence of Jesus of Nazareth.[16]

Taken together these facts argue for the basic reliability of the Gospel record. It can indeed be asserted in the words of Bishop Stephen Neill that

The Jesus Christ ... who is made present in the proclamation of the Gospel ... is the same Jesus who was born at a specific time and place in history, who lived a human life, who spoke certain words, did certain deeds and suffered certain things of which we have clear though far from complete knowledge.[17]

2 Reasons for Doubt?

Views which oppose the reliability of the gospel record are numerous and therefore the present discussion is confined to two prominent ones which any student of the New Testament will undoubtedly encounter. Firstly there are views which oppose the reliability of the gospel record because of the way it was formed. Secondly, there are views which oppose the reliability of the gospel records because of its content and meaning.

Unreliable because of the way it was formed

One of the significant milestones in Gospel criticism was B. H. Streeter's Four Document hypothesis which first appeared in his book the *Four Gospels,* published in 1924. In outline Streeter argued that Mark was the earliest of the four Gospels. Matthew and Luke then made use of Mark and another source generally referred to as 'Q', 'Q' being the first letter of the German word 'Quelle' meaning source. The existence of 'Q' was posited largely on the basis that Matthew and Luke have a substantial body of common material not found in Mark. Streeter also concluded that Matthew alone had access to a sayings source which he designated 'M', whilst the third evangelist only used a corpus of material designated 'L' which appeared to come from Caesarea.

The majority of New Testament scholars still accept and work on the basis of Streeter's hypothesis. However, by the early 1930s another development known as 'Form Criticism' had appeared on the scene. In the source criticism of Streeter and others, work centred around the use of Mark and 'Q' by Matthew and Luke. Source criticism could not push the study behind these fairly substantial documents. The most it could do was to posit an earlier form of Mark's Gospel. The 'form critics' however set themselves to study the origin of both Mark and 'Q'. Within these documents they analysed according to their 'form' different types of material and arrived at categories such as 'parables', 'miracles', 'stories', 'sayings', 'legends', and so forth. According to the form critics, information about the life and ministry of Jesus circulated in these smaller units or 'forms' of tradition which arose largely in response to the needs of the first Christians. Thus, for example, the early Christians experienced persecution or problems over paying tribute so they collected together their Master's sayings on these matters.

Form critics have helped us in our understanding of the origin of the gospel material. However they, like the rest of us, bring challengeable assumptions to their reading of the Gospels and it is arguable that these are less defensible than those of the historicists. According to the form critics the needs of the church came first and foremost, and the actual chronicling of the life of Jesus was only a secondary concern. Furthermore form critics generally assume that these forms did not emerge until after the events of Easter. The compilation and selection of these forms, it is argued, were made from a standpoint of commitment and, therefore, they must display a bias.

The result of these two assumed tendencies is that much, or at least some, of the detail of Jesus' life and teaching has been distorted. What, therefore, we find written in the pages of the New Testament is not altogether reliable in that it clearly cannot accurately convey the facts as they were.

A more radical approach

Some of the more radical form critics are prepared to carry the matter considerably further. For such, not only were the events in the life and teaching of Jesus obscured in the way we have indicated, they were deliberately and consciously altered. Bultmann, for example, suggests that miracle stories resulted from 'dramatisations' by the disciples of the sayings of Jesus. Thus, the incident in John's Gospel in which a blind man was healed was simply a piece of literary license to illustrate the saying that Jesus is the light of the world. Similarly the withering of the fig tree was merely an embellishment to add significance to the parable of the barren fig tree.

Bultmann, in particular, goes on to point out that the miracle stories reveal the same style and structure as the stories of miracles in Hellenistic sources. In his *Study of the Synoptic Gospels* he writes:

The following seem to be characteristic of the style observed in the narrative of miracles. As a rule the narrative is given in three parts. First, the condition of the patient is described. Just as, for example, in Mark 9:18 we read, 'I have brought unto thee my son who hath a dumb spirit; and wheresoever he taketh him, he teareth him: and he foameth and gnasheth with his teeth and pineth away' – so Lucian tells the story (*Philopseudes* = The Friend of Lies C.16) of a certain 'Syrian from Palestine', a 'wise man' who had understanding in these matters: he was known to have healed many, 'who fell down in fits, rolled their eyes, and foamed at the mouth'. Typical also is the emphasis upon the gravity of the illness (e.g. Mark 5:3–5) or its long duration (e.g. Mark 5:25f; 9:12; Luke 13:11). Just as in the Greek stories, so Mark 5:26 describes the futile efforts of the physicians to heal the illness, and also the scornful attitude of the people when the true healer first appeared (Mark 5:40). Just as here it is said that the crowd standing about the house of mourning laughed Jesus to scorn, so, for example, the inscriptions in the temple of the healing God Asclepios at Epidauros tell of a sick woman who laughed sceptically when she heard of the marvellous deeds of the God, or how the crowd ridiculed the folly of a man totally blind who hoped for divine healing.

In the second section of the story the healing itself is narrated. Often the peculiar manipulations of the healer are described, as in Mark 7:33; 8:23. . . . In Hellenistic stories we are told, for example, how an exorcist drove the spirit out of a demoniac by holding a ring to the patient's nose so that he might smell a marvellous root that has been set in it: or how another healed a person of snake-bite by placing upon the wounded foot a tiny piece of the gravestone of a virgin, to the accompaniment of an appropriate magic formula. In the gospels as a rule it is simply stated, as likewise in the Hellenestic narratives, that the wonder worker approaches the patient – perhaps coming to his bedside – lays his hand upon him or takes him by the hand and utters the healing word. It is also characteristic that these words are as a rule given in an unknown foreign tongue, like 'Talitha Kumi' (Mark 5:41) and 'Ephphatha' (Mark 7:34). . . .

Two characteristics are found in the third section, as a rule. First of all it was naturally often pointed out that witnesses of the wonderful results of the miracles broke out in exclamations of wonder or approval. . . . Following the exorcism of demons the demonstration often consists in some spiteful and destructive act of the departing demon, like the shattering of a pillar or the overturning of a bowl of water, or, as in Mark 5:13, the sudden frenzy of a herd of swine who dash over a cliff and fall into the sea.[1]

From this fact that the miracle stories in the Gospels are written in exactly the same stylised form as the miracles attributed to the Hellenistic wonder-workers such as the pagan Apollonius of Tyana, Bultmann concludes that they must, therefore, be regarded as fabrications. However, there is a fallacy in this argument. The fact that all the miracles in the gospels are written up in a stylised form does not, therefore, prove them to be fictional. For example, most medical case histories today are written up in a standard format but that does not therefore prove them to be inaccurate. Similarly in the local newspapers weddings are often reported in the same monotonous fashion: 'The wedding of Mr. X and Miss Y took place at —. The bride, who was given away by her father Mr. Y, wore —' and so forth. The form critics may be right in asserting that the form in which the New Testament miracle stories are written was typical of the first century and can be paralleled in Hellenistic literature, but they make a false deduction when they assert them for that reason to be fabrications. It should be pointed out that some scholars such as H. Riesenfeld have demonstrated that the symbolism of all the New Testament miracles can be found in the Old Testament and Judaism[2] and therefore we need not necessarily suppose them to be modelled on Hellenistic miracle stories.

Form critics have similarly asserted that the other forms in which the account of Jesus' life and ministry is preserved are, like the miracles, not to be taken as having a substance of historical fact. This can be illustrated in the following four assertions by leading form critical scholars. Bultmann again, writing in *Jesus and the Word,* says: 'I do indeed think that we can know almost nothing concerning the life and personality of Jesus since the early Christian sources show no interest in either, are more fragmentary and often legendary; and other sources about Jesus do not exist'.[3] Professor Norman Perrin in *Rediscovering the Teaching of Jesus* suggests that many of the narratives in the Gospels have been freely created within the early church, and that 'the most that the present writer believes can be claimed for a Gospel narrative is that it may represent a typical scene from the ministry of Jesus'.[4]

In the introduction to his Pelican commentary on *Saint Mark* Professor Dennis Nineham says of the Gospel writers: 'Their attitude to historical and biographical accuracy was ... even by the standards of their own day ... popular rather than scholarly'.[5] And in this rather longer quotation from Professor John Macquarrie's *Principles of Christian Theology* we have a very clear indication of the way in which form critics believe the historical Jesus has been totally lost to us:

> The researches of form-criticism have made it clear that the Jesus of history has, to a much greater extent than hitherto recognised, slipped beyond the horizon of what we can know, and that the figure presented in the gospels, and the incidents concerning him are, to say the least, strongly coloured by the faith and teaching of the early church. The historical, human Jesus has, in the thought of the church, been transformed into the supernatural Christ whose setting is not historical but mythical. ... The story of Jesus in the gospels is told in the light of this conception of the supernatural Christ, and the beliefs of the Church about Jesus as the Christ have been read back into the story of his life.[6]

These scholars and others like them, asserted that because the documents are written after the Easter events by a believing community, they are therefore biased or to use Macquarrie's words 'strongly coloured'. So much is this so 'that the historical Jesus has in the thought of the Church, been transformed into the supernatural Christ whose setting is not historical but mythical'. On this view, the New Testament is historically unreliable. How convincing are the arguments underlying it?

Three Objections

First, it would seem that many of those who use this argument that the disciples' stories were coloured by the Easter faith are trying 'to have their cake and eat it'. Bultmann, for example, is unwilling to assert that the resurrection is an historical event in which Christ actually rose bodily from the tomb. For him it is rather a mythological way of presenting the deeply felt significance of his death.[7] But unless one is prepared to assert that Christ rose from the dead there is hardly a sufficient motivating force for the writing of accounts of an obscure Galilean carpenter and peripatetic teacher who clashed with the authorities after only three years and was executed for his pains.

Furthermore, in response to Bultmann's so-called 'Christian Imagination Theory' we must ask with Canon Michael Green: 'Who among his disciples or among their proselytes was capable of inventing the sayings of Jesus or imagining the life and character revealed in the Gospels?'[8] Certainly not the fishermen of Galilee or Levi, the tax collector. Which of these men who had been so deeply impressed by the man Jesus Christ were capable of writing such profound theology so as to obscure totally the historicity?

To change the tack of the argument for a moment, perhaps it is apposite to ask whether it is really likely that the Easter faith generates such bias that it is no longer possible to see the facts of Christian history with basic objectivity? Christian people today live by the same Easter faith as Luke or the Apostle Paul but does that mean we are no longer able accurately to recount the facts of Christian history in which we have a part?

How close to the events?

One of the great weaknesses of form criticism is that it has failed to take sufficient account of the fact that the finished gospels appeared at a point in time comparatively close to the events which they describe. This necessarily means that there must have been many eye-witnesses still alive at the time of publication who would have acted as a safeguard against fabrication.

J. A. T. Robinson in his *Redating of the New Testament* describes this period between the events of the life, death and resurrection of Jesus and the period of writing as the 'tunnel period' at the end of which the train emerges, laden with the baggage of ecclesiastical language. Obviously, says Robinson, the shorter the tunnel or period between the events and writing, the less is the likelihood of there being a distortion.[9] The significant fact about Robinson's work is that his redating of the New Testament makes for a considerably shorter 'tunnel period' than most scholars have traditionally allowed. In fact, Robinson now puts almost all the New Testament documents before A.D. 70. This means that the gap between the events described and the time of writing is of the order of a mere 35 years. In a period of three decades we are still well within the limits of living memory. Thus, when the Gospels first appeared there were many people still alive who could test the author of Luke-Acts' claim to have written 'an orderly accurate account'.[10]

It is interesting that Tacitus wrote what is generally regarded as accurate history of the reigns of Tiberius to Nero from between 45 to 80 years after the events while many theologians assert that the New Testament writers produced almost total distortions a mere 35 years after the events. Tacitus, it may be countered, is believed because the events he describes are commonplace rather than supernatural and are therefore credible. On the other hand the substantial historicity of much in Homer is not impugned because of the supernatural trimmings. It is indeed astonishing that ancient historians are more willing to allow the Homeric poems, which were written several hundred years after the event, to teach them what happened in the Trojan War than some scholars are to allow the Gospels, which were written in living memory of the event, to teach them about the life and work of Jesus.

At times all these arguments and counter arguments seem very abstruse so perhaps it is appropriate to conclude this discussion in slightly lighter vein with a quotation which John Robinson draws from A. H. N. Green-Armytage:

There is a world – I do not say a world in which all scholars live but one at any rate into which all of them sometimes stray, and which some of them seem permanently to inhabit – which is not the world in which I live. In my world, if *The Times* and *The Telegraph* both tell one story in somewhat different terms, nobody concludes that one of them must have copied the other, nor that the variations in the story have some esoteric significance. But in that world of which I am speaking this would be taken for granted. There, no story is ever derived from the facts but always from somebody else's version of the same story.

   ... In my world, almost every book, except some of those produced by Government departments, is written by one author. In that world almost every book is produced by a committee, and some of them by a whole series of committees. In my world, if I read Mr. Churchill, in 1935, said that Europe was heading for a disastrous war, I applaud his foresight. In that world they say, 'The World War narrative took shape in the third decade of the twentieth century'. In my world men and women live for a considerable time – seventy, eighty, even a hundred years – and they are equipped with a thing called memory. In that world (it would appear) they come into being, write a book, and forthwith perish, all in a flash, and it is noted with astonishment that they 'preserve traces of primitive tradition' about things which happened well within their own adult lifetime.[11]

Our second category of views which oppose the reliability of the Gospel Record claim it is

Unreliable because of its Content and Meaning

This second important argument against the trustworthiness of the Gospels is concerned, not with the process by which the information came to be written down, but rather with the problem of its *meaning.* The issue is one of interpretation and in particular the ability to distinguish between 'truth' and 'literal truth'. This is a distinction which we are all used to making in our daily conversation when we use such phrases as: 'He's a pig', 'She's a doll' or, 'I've just lost my head'. These are phrases which we can accept as true and yet they are not 'literally' true. Rather strangely perhaps, when we come to the statements in the biblical literature we find the distinction a little harder to make.

What is a myth?

Part of the reason for this difficulty may lie in the term 'myth' which is often employed as a technical term to designate certain figurative statements. The word 'myth' as it is popularly used, however, is taken to mean something which is not true. The exclamation: 'That's a myth' is generally another way of saying: 'That's a lie'.

Among theologians there is no general consensus of opinion as to the meaning and scope of the term 'myth'. Some limit 'myth' to representations of the transcendent in earthly terms while others use it to cover anything which is couched in symbolic or pictorial language. It is because of this diversity of view that Bishop Stephen Neill has described myth as a 'quicksilver' term.

G. B. Caird's definition of myth would perhaps be acceptable to a fairly wide range of scholars. Caird defines myth as 'a pictorial way of expressing truths which cannot be expressed so readily or so forcefully in any other way'. Caird in fact emphasizes that myth is not to be confused with legend or fairy tale. I think it would be adequate to state therefore that generally a 'myth' has two aspects:

1. It is a statement of 'truth as opposed to 'literal truth', and

2. It is a statement in pictorial language. The key to recognition of myth in this sense in the biblical narrative is obviously the use of the pictorial language.

Using this understanding it might be helpful to look at one or two examples from the New Testament documents. In Matthew 5:34–35 we find Christ's injunction: 'But I say unto you, Do not swear at all, either by heaven, for it is the throne of God, or by earth, for it is his footstool'. Clearly we are not intended to deduce that God literally sits in heaven with his feet on the earth. Jesus' words are simply intended to express the truth that in the heavenly realm God's will is perfectly fulfilled whilst although in earthly kingdoms God's will is not acknowledged, they are still under his rule. Another example might be in Matthew 11:23 where Jesus says: 'And you, Capernaum, will you be exalted to heaven? You shall be brought down to Hades'. Once again we are not intended to assert a cosmology with heaven 'up' and 'hell' down below. Clearly that runs into difficulties because on that basis heaven for the person at the North Pole would be in the same direction as hell for the person at the South Pole! Obviously hell is not in depths underneath the ground we tread. No, all that Jesus intended to indicate was two levels of existence, one infinitely superior to the other.

Another example might be the doctrine of Christ's session as it is taught in Hebrews 10:12 and other passages. In these Christ is depicted as 'sitting at God's right hand'. In such contexts, the New Testament is using pictorial language drawn from the Oriental Court, perhaps indeed from the Judean court alluded to in Psalm 110, in which the chief minister or official sat on the right hand of the monarch. The writer does not intend us to understand that Father and Son literally sit all day on a pair of adjacent thrones in a distant heavenly location. Nevertheless the picture expresses the 'truth' that Christ is now in the place of supreme authority.

Demythologising

In each of these examples, what we have done is simply to interpret the language in order to highlight the truth which it conveys. This is a process which Bultmann calls 'demythologising'. To 'demythologise' passages of scripture, according to Bultmann, is 'to make them understandable to modern thought. Demythologising ... is a method of interpreting scripture'.[13] Thus far, most can agree with Bultmann. The great divide however occurs because he, and others like him, not only appear to 'demythologise' or re-interpret the pictorial language, but also in many cases seek to re-interpret the truth which that language is intended to convey. In other words, they throw out the baby with the bath water. A great deal of contemporary Christology falls into this error and, therefore, amounts to a subtle undermining of the reliability of the biblical text.

Perhaps by way of conclusion an illustration from the recent volume, *The Myth of God Incarnate*, might help to clarify the point. Professor Hick recognizes that the 'incarnation' is a special category of myth in that it is tied to a datable historical event. Most of us, however, would probably want to maintain that the language surrounding the doctrine is not mythological at all but rather metaphysical. Hick asks, 'What would be compatible with affirming the incarnation myth in relation to Jesus?' He then proceeds to answer his own question.

> We would want, I suppose, to be able to affirm two things. First that his own life in its relation to God embodied ... openness to God ... and secondly that ... in his attitudes towards other men his life was a parable of the loving outreach of God to the world.

In his efforts to 'demythologise' or 'interpret' the meaning of the language, Hick has clearly separated himself from mainstream Christian belief formulated at Nicea asserting that God was in Christ and that Jesus was both fully God and fully human from birth.[15] Such an assertion in the view of many scholars, to say nothing of legions of less distinguished Christians down through the ages, is implicit in the New Testament and even comes to explicit statement in some passages (see for example 2 Corinthians 5:19) which have to be explained away by this school.

In another essay Hick again writes in similar vein:

> I see the Nazarene, then, as intensely and overwhelmingly conscious of the reality of God. He was a man of God ... His Spirit was open to God and his life a continuous response to the divine love (as both utterly gracious and utterly demanding). He was so powerfully God-conscious that his life vibrated as it were, to the divine life; and as a result his hands could heal the sick, and the 'poor in spirit' were kindled to new life in his presence.

Before such a man, says Hick, 'we might have found ourselves trembling or in tears or uttering the strange sounds that are today called speaking in tongues'.[16] (In this context, at least, it seems that Pentecost has so far escaped the demythologisation treatment!)

Demythologising the gospel stories, in an attempt to convey their 'real' meaning without supernatural associations, may seem an attractive way of securing their credibility and relevance. But it is important to preserve the basic and central truth enshrined within the symbol or picture.

3. The Importance of the Historical Jesus

Some readers may still be uncertain about whether the historicity of the Gospels matters a great deal. Could Christianity not survive if it were proved that Jesus never really lived or that (assuming he did live) we have no reliable information about him?

Rooted in history

Christianity is not merely a religion, it is a religion which is rooted in history. It makes its appeal to something which can be dated. '... when Quirinius was governor ... she gave birth to her first born son'[1] and 'Pilate gave sentence that their demand should be granted'.[2] It is possible never to have heard of great Hindu teachers such as Sankara or Ramanuja and still be a perfectly good Hindu, but Christianity, like Buddhism and Islam is a historical religion; the events of its beginning can be dated.

However for Christianity the historical facts relating to its founder are crucial in a way that is not true for either Buddhism or Islam. In neither of these is the central doctrine of salvation dependent upon any connexion with events in the life of either the Buddha or Muhammad. In contrast, in Christianity the emphasis is not on things which Jesus said, but on certain things which God actually did. Therefore Christians are deeply committed to an interest in history. As one of the contributors to the *Myth of God Incarnate* succinctly puts it: 'He who says "Jesus" says also 'history',[3] or as A. S. Peake stated it writing about the turn of the century: 'Christianity professes to be a religion rooted in time and history'.[4]

The Christian faith makes an unmistakeable link between the truths which it claims and certain events which happened in space and time: supremely that God came into the world of men in the person of Jesus Christ, that Jesus Christ died for our sins and was buried and rose again on the third day. The question is therefore raised at once; 'Did those events really happen or not?'

We live in a pragmatic age in which men and women want to know if Jesus really existed and whether he was the kind of person the Gospels make him out to be. People want to know if Christ's teaching really was supported by his personal behaviour. If the life of Jesus presented to us in the Gospels can be asserted then we know that the Christian way of life is not a utopian dream but something which has a note of reality to it. It is something which is possible for ordinary everyday people. Twentieth century man lives in a real world, his interest is not gripped by a Jesus who belongs to a mythical cult like Mithras or Attis, he is looking for a Jesus who has the ring of truth about him. Such a Jesus can only be the historical Jesus.

What do you mean: 'historical'?

The question is, what do we mean by the 'historical Jesus'? Here we need to distinguish between the terms 'historical' and 'historic'. The word 'historical' describes things which 'actually happened'. The word 'historic' describes events which have significance. Some famous words associated with Martin Luther, 'Here I stand, I can do no other, so help me God', may not be 'historical' in the sense that he personally actually said them, but as Roland Bainton and other Reformation scholars have pointed out, they are 'historic' in that they perfectly express the significance of the events at the Diet of Worms and show how subsequent Protestants interpreted Luther.

A number of historians have taken the view that for something to be 'historical' it must contain the 'bare facts' without any interpretation or colouring from the reporter's pen: 'Nottingham Forest won the 1978 League Cup by a goal to nil. The goal was scored by Robertson.' That statement is the bare substance of an event. Now it might be possible to go on to state that it was a well-taken goal which was deserved, but once such a statement is made, an interpretation has been placed on the facts. Many scholars would still be prepared to accept such an interpretation as 'historical' although clearly we are now on slightly softer ground. Most of this discussion about the 'historical Jesus' which follows is therefore related to 'historical' in the first 'bare facts' sense.

Having established a meaning for the term 'historical Jesus', it is now possible to examine the available evidence for the historical Jesus. What is there in the Gospels which can be asserted as 'historical'?

The Evidence for the Historical Jesus

The historical Jesus died and was buried and then on the third day came alive again and entered the heavenly sphere and thus became the contemporary Christ. In I. H. Marshall's words: 'The result of this is that the Jesus of history and the Christ of faith are one and the same person, or rather the same person at two stages in his career.[5]

We have noted a tendency for New Testament scholars to try to drive a wedge between the 'Jesus of History' and the 'Christ of Faith'. Yet the New Testament writers appear to be conscious that the Lord in whom they have faith and whom they proclaimed in their preaching was the same Jesus who walked by Galilee and shared their toils and sorrows. In fact, Peter in his sermon on the Day of Pentecost makes this link very clearly (Acts 2:36): 'This Jesus whom you crucified (the historical Jesus) God has made both Lord and Christ (the Christ of Faith)'.

We have seen already on the basis of factors such as the existence of eye-witnesses and the retentiveness of oriental memory that the evidence for the historicity of the Gospels is good. In spite of this, some people may remain unwilling to accept these arguments. But in recent years a number of scholars have shown that by applying different principles to the New Testament documents themselves, it is *still* possible to reconstruct a range of historical facts about Jesus.

The more radical among the form critics have set up a number of criteria by which they urge it is possible to assert that certain features of the life and teaching of Jesus are historical.[7] There is, for instance, the criterion of 'dissimilarity'. According to this principle a saying can be regarded as certainly authentic only if it can be shown to be dissimilar to the characteristic emphasis of both ancient Judaism and the early church. A good example of the use of this criterion is seen in Jesus' address of God as 'Abba'-Father. This was not the way in which Old Testament Jews addressed God and it is found only twice in early church usage. The great weakness of this criterion is that it is necessarily very limited. It is quite obvious that much of what Jesus taught must have become an integral part of early church teaching.

A second criterion is that of 'multiple attestation'. Where an incident or a piece of teaching is found in more than one of the earliest Gospel sources established by critical study, it can be said that there is some guarantee that it goes back to Jesus. An example of this is the saying of Jesus about saving one's life and losing it which occurs in Mark, 'Q' and a source used by John.

Another such criterion is the criterion of 'unintentionality'. The early church, it is argued, was careful to preserve tradition which emphasised Jesus' supernatural character as the one who had come from God, yet at some points aspects of the humanity of Jesus still shine through the Gospel record. These, it is suggested, must have been unintentionally overlooked and left in the accounts of Jesus' life. A notable example of this would be Jesus' attitude to women which Professor C. F. D. Moule refers to in *The Phenomenon of the New Testament:*

How comes it that, through all the gospel traditions wihout exception, there comes a remarkably firmly-drawn portrait of an attractive young man moving freely about among women of all sorts, including the decidedly disreputable ... yet at every point, maintaining a simple integrity of character?[8]

The other criteria of this type which are used similarly are the criterion of 'coherence' and the criterion of 'traditional continuity'. The criterion of 'coherence' asserts that material may be regarded as authentic if it 'coheres' or agrees with material which has already been established as 'historical' by means of the criterion of 'dissimilarity'. The criterion of 'traditional continuity' argues that each statement or story about Jesus which is established as authentic by means of any of the other four criteria must continue from, or have its basis in, an actual saying or action of Jesus.

Any saying that satisfies these criteria can almost certainly be regarded as authentic so that even by these means a great deal of support can be gained for the traditional picture of the sayings of Jesus. Such a picture however is unnecessarily restrictive in respect of any attempt to build up an overall picture and clearly we can move beyond these limits. A. R. C. Leaney in his essay entitled 'Historicity in the Gospels' which appears in *Vindications* writes: 'The intention of the gospels, whether realised or not, is to present the Lord of Salvation as historical.'[9] He continues: 'It is an indispensable part of their message to insist that he is to be identified with a certain local craftsman who was registered in the Roman Census'.[10]

Leaney further points out that what offended Jesus' fellow townsmen was that they had to identify this remarkable person with 'someone they had known as historically as we know our next-door neighbours'.[11] (See Mark 6:1–6)

Using Leaney's essay as a basis, but drawing on the work of one or two other writers it is possible to assert that other features in the Gospel accounts have the likelihood of being historical.

The names of various places which are recorded as being centres of Jesus' ministry may reasonably be accepted as historical. Nazareth was situated in the northern part of Lower Galilee and any man with a mission would naturally make his way to the busy centres of Capernaum, Chorazin and Bethsaida.

The opposition of Jesus' family (Mark 3:21) is an historical fact which is frequently overlooked. It might be objected that this is a theological point ('He came to his own and his own did not accept him') represented as historical. However Luke (in 2:51) indicates that there was a period when the relationship between Jesus and his family was agreeable. Furthermore a falsified version of the matter would be more likely to depict Jesus as a local success. And if a ministry in Galilee can be accepted as historical, then the journey to Jerusalem cannot be dismissed on the ground that it has nothing but theological significance as Hans Conzelmann and others have argued.[12]

Passages which show the apostles/Twelve in a bad light are likely to be historical. Mark would have been unlikely to have invented material which was disparaging to the honour of the apostles. Typical instances of this are the occasion when Jesus explained his forthcoming sufferings and the disciples took fear,[13] and the incident in which the sons of Zebedee sought prominent places in the coming Kingdom.

Regarding the miracles, Leaney makes the point that no-one – not even the bitterest opponents of those early days – attempted to deny the fact reported by the evangelists that Jesus did possess miraculous powers. They simply attempted to discredit them by ascribing them to an evil source. Leaney writes: 'In marked contrast to the miracles in the Old Testament, which are taken for granted and told without embarrassment, those narrated by the Evangelists cause great astonishment and are as far as possible concealed by Jesus himself'.[15]

Complaints against Jesus associating with outcasts would also seem to be historical. Admittedly, such incidents could have been invented to explain the Church's preoccupation with 'unclean' people – 'sinners' and Samaritan Gentiles – but it needs to be remembered that the early church soon found itself forced out into a mission to the Gentiles. The reproach was therefore something the early church would not have felt.

The claim of Christ to divinity has been put down as hagiography but this cannot be allowed to pass as a satisfactory explanation. Christ's claim to equality with God and to have authority to forgive sin is one of the irreducible minima of the Gospel story. What other satisfactory explanation is there for the hatred and anger of the Jewish leaders, the indictment of blasphemy and the various attempts to liquidate him?

Regarding the crucifixion we can confidently assert that no serious scholar would be prepared to deny its factuality. To do so would be to question the very historicity of Jesus himself and everything which concerns him.

This is not the place to argue for the historical fact of the resurrection but let it be said that the evidence for this position far outweighs the other possibilities as Michael Green and George Ladd have demonstrated.[16] It is significant that the disciples were at first sceptical about their Lord's resurrection and then when he was seen by them it was usually at moments when they were not expecting him. When however they came to set their resurrection narratives into writing, they insist that the risen Jesus was the 'same' historical Jesus they had known, lived and worked with: 'See my hands and my feet, that it is I myself; handle me, and see; for a spirit has not flesh and bones as you see that I have'[17]

The evidence for accepting the Gospels as reliable historical evidence is solid, as we saw previously, and the committed Christian need have no qualms in viewing them as such. Yet nevertheless, even working with these methods of inquiry, it is possible to establish the basic and essential historical facts concerning the ministry and teaching of Jesus.

How important is the historicity of Jesus?

It has already been indicated that certainty about the historical Jesus is a vital concern for the Christian but there is more to be said on the matter.

1. Basic for New Testament Teaching

If the 'historical Jesus' is unimportant we have to ask ourselves why do we need the Gospels? Surely the rest of the New Testament would be adequate for our needs? Yet if we believe in the incarnation we are compelled to ask what reasons there are for believing that the incarnation took place in Jesus.

So much of what Jesus taught is dependent on certain historical acts which he accomplished in his life and ministry; Jesus taught that 'God is love', but how can we know that God is a loving God and Father if he has not revealed himself in Jesus Christ? If there is no event, where do we derive this idea of God as a loving Father from? To bring the issue to a more personal level, the doctrine of the love of God is very difficult to accept in the face of pain and misery. But the Christian can look to *history* to reinforce him in his assurance of God's love. We can assert that God loves in all situations including those of suffering because he actually demonstrated his love in history to the full and in every kind of human situation. The historical scheme in which Christianity is set would therefore seem to provide an objective point of reference with which the subjective experience of faith can be compared. Apart from such an historical framework faith would have to seek some other way of making itself intelligible.

To take another example, the doctrine of salvation can be cited. Peter assures his Christian readers that the wholeness which they know results from the historical fact that 'Christ himself bore our sins on the tree'. Paul in both of his letters to the Christians at Corinth guarantees their resurrection on the ground of the historical fact of Jesus' resurrection. In 2 Corinthians 4 he writes: 'We too believe ... knowing that he who raised the Lord Jesus will raise us'. In 1 Corinthians 15 the issue is even more clear-cut: 'If Christ has not been raised, the dead are not raised. If Christ has not been raised your faith is futile and you are still in your sins'

It has been argued that the empty tomb is a late tradition created as a necessary corollary to the appearances of the risen Lord. However, this can be countered by the fact that the earliest preaching (see 1 Corinthians 15:4) believed something that happened the third day which had not happened earlier.

We can summarise by saying that central to the New Testament is the fact that it is not the message itself which saves men and women but the historical events of Jesus' life, death and resurrection of which the message merely speaks. This is why again and again in the recorded instances of preaching in the New Testament Church the apostles conclude by making appeal to the historical Jesus: 'This Jesus whom you crucified God has made Lord and Christ' '... it was by the name of Jesus Christ of Nazareth, whom you crucified, whom God raised from the dead; it is by his name that this man stands before you fit and well'.[19] For the New Testament, salvation depends totally on verifiable facts.

The presupposition, indeed the argument, of so many form-critical scholars, is that we cannot find the historical Jesus in the pages of the New Testament. The Apostolic community, they say, was not concerned about this issue. Yet when we actually turn to the pages of the New Testament documents we find on the contrary that the writers have an emphatic concern to present the historical Jesus and to link their teaching with him. Peter emphasises the point at the beginning of his second letter.

> We have not depended on made-up stories in making known to you the mighty coming of our Lord Jesus Christ. With our own eyes we saw his greatness. We were there when he was given honour and glory by the Father, when the voice came to him from the Supreme Glory, saying, 'This is my own dear son, with whom I am pleased!' We ourselves heard this voice coming from heaven, when we were with him on the holy mountain.[20]

Similarly John begins his first letter in the following way.

> We write to you about the Word of life which has existed from the very beginning. We have heard it, and we have seen it with our eyes; yes, we have seen it, and our hands have touched it ... so we speak of it and tell you about the eternal life which was with the Father and was made known to us.[21]

2. Basic for New Testament Faith

Not only is the fact of the 'historical Jesus' important because New Testament teaching is dependent on it, it is also important because New Testament faith is dependent on it.

At the very heart of the New Testament is

the doctrine that we are made acceptable to God on the ground of our faith in Jesus Christ. But faith can spring up and grow within us only if we use our minds. The Psalmist said, 'Those who know thy name put their trust in thee'.[22] In other words trust springs from knowledge of the trustworthiness of God's character. Paul writes in Romans 12 that our commitment to Christ includes the area of our mind. Faith (if it is to be faith rather than folly) must have a basis of reason. To maintain that the historicity of Jesus is unimportant means that we are left with an insufficient basis for New Testament faith. W. A. Whitehouse writing on ' "Faith" in the New Testament' points out that the word implies 'reasoned knowledge'.[24] To go further and to maintain, as some form critics do, that it would not matter if Jesus' bones were unearthed in Palestine and that Jesus lives on in other ways in the memory and teaching of the Christian church, is to make New Testament faith an impossibility. For as Whitehouse goes on to show,[25] New Testament faith always has its focus in a person. To imply that one can exercise faith in a memory which lives on in the Church cannot do justice to the meaning of the biblical terminology.

3. Basic for New Testament Experience

The danger of stressing experience of the living Christ with whom we have immediate fellowship and paying little attention to the historical Jesus of the Gospels is that we soon begin to devise a Christian experience of our own making. In the words of Arthur Samuel Peake, a Methodist theologian at the beginning of the present century: 'A Christianity disentangled from the Gospel facts has ceased to be Christianity in any real sense of the term'.[26] It comes instead to be what Peake terms 'a religion of cloud-land'.[27] If we were to transport a man from the Outer Hebrides to New York City, then unless that man were to keep in regular touch with his roots by frequently journeying back to his homeland he would rapidly cease to bear any resemblance to the Hebrideans in his attitudes, values and life-style. Similarly if we cut our Christian experience loose from its root in the historical Jesus, it will very rapidly become a totally subjective affair and lack any resemblance to the experience of its founder. It is therefore crucial that we keep the historical Jesus in the forefront of our thinking and that we re-appraise our every experience and our every doctrine in the light of his experiences and his teachings. In fact, when John in his first letter urges us to 'test' or 'examine' every spiritual experience the standard we are to use is the standard of the historical Jesus.[28]

Knowledge of the historical Jesus is something that Christianity cannot dispense with. Whatever sort of 'Jesus-religion' may be possible without such knowledge, it can be called Christianity only in some limited and qualified manner.

That is why it is so important that Christians of the twentieth century should be able to make with a confidence that is based on knowledge the affirmation of 2 Peter 3:16:

We have not depended on made-up legends in making known to you the mighty coming of our Lord Jesus Christ.

NOTES

Chapter One

1. R. H. Lightfoot, 'The Critical Approach to the Bible in the Nineteenth Century' *The Interpretation of the Bible* (London, S.P.C.K., 1944) p. 75f
2. N. E. Perrin, *Rediscovering the Teaching of Jesus* (New York, 1967) p. 208
3. P. S. Minear *Commands of Christ* (Edinburgh, 1972) p. 21
4. E. Käsemann, *Essays on New Testament Themes* (S.C.M., 1964) p. 46
5. See T. W. Manson, *Studies in the Gospels and Epistles* (Philadelphia, Westminster Press, 1962) pp. 28–45, 65–87
6. D. Guthrie 'Form Criticism and its Developments' *New Testament Introduction* (London, Tyndale Press, 3rd edn., 1970) p. 228
7. *Ibid.*
8. *Ibid.*
9. V. Taylor, *The Gospels: A Short Introduction* p. 12
10. D. Guthrie, *op. cit.,* p.225, note 1.
11. See D. Cupitt, *Who was Jesus?* (B.B.C., 1978)
12. Eusebius, *Ecclesiastical History* iii; 39:15
13. See A. M. Hunter, *According to John* (S.C.M., 1968) p. 51
14. W. Ramsay, *St. Paul: Traveller and Roman Citizen* p. 222
15. I. H. Marshall *Luke: Historian and Theologian* (Exeter, Paternoster Press, 1970) p. 69
16. For these references see M. Tenney, *New*

Testament Survey (London, Tyndale Press, 1967) pp. 199–201
17. S. Neill, Foreword to Heinz Zahnt, *The Historical Jesus*

Chapter Two

1. R. Bultmann, *Form Criticism* (Harper & Row, 1962) pp. 37–39. Copyright 1934 by Willett, Clark and Co. Renewed copyright 1962 by Frederick C. Grant
2. H. Riesenfeld, *The Gospel Tradition and Its Beginning* (Mowbray, 1957) p. 9
3. R. Bultmann, *Jesus and the Word* (1934) p. 8
4. N. Perrin, *Rediscovering the Teaching of Jesus* (S.C.M., 1967) p. 29
5. D. Nineham, *Saint Mark* (Pelican, 1963) p. 49
6. J. Macquarrie, *Principles of Christian Theology* (S.C.M., 1977) p. 274
7. See *R. Bultmann,* (ed.) E. J. Tinsley (Epworth, 1973) pp. 73–78
8. See (ed.) M. Green, *The Truth of God Incarnate* (Hodder, 1977) ch. 6
9. J. A. T. Robinson, *Redating the New Testament* (S.C.M., 1976) p. 355
10. Luke 1:13
11. J. A. T. Robinson *op. cit.,* p. 356, citing A. H. N. Green-Armytage, *John Who Saw* (1952) p. 12f
12. G. B. Caird, *St. Luke* (Penguin, 1963) p. 79
13. E. J. Tinsley (ed.), *Rudolf Bultmann* (London, Epworth, 1973) p. 64
14. J. Hick (ed.), *The Myth of God Incarnate* (S.C.M., 1977) p. 162
15. J. Hick (ed.), *op. cit.,* p. 172
16. J. Hick (ed.), *loc. cit.*

Chapter Three

1. Luke 2:2 and 7

2. Luke 23:24
3. *The Myth of God Incarnate* (ed.) J. Hick (S.C.M., 1977) p. 71
4. Peake, A. S., *Christianity its Nature and its Truth* (Duckworth, 1907) p. 139
5. I. H. Marshall, *I Believe in the Historical Jesus* (Hodder, 1977) p. 61
6. Acts 2:36
7. N. Perrin, *Rediscovering the Teaching of Jesus* (S.C.M., 1967) pp. 36–46
8. C. F. D. Moule, *The Phenomenon of the New Testament* (S.C.M., 1967) pp. 63f
9. A. Hanson (ed.) *Vindications* (S.C.M., 1966) p. 115
10. *Ibid.* p. 115
11. *Ibid.* p. 115
12. H. Conzelmann, *The Theology of St. Luke* (London, Faber & Faber, 1960) p. 19f
13. Mark 10:32a
14. Mark 10:35–45
15. A Hanson (ed.) *op. cit.,* p. 123
16. See G. Ladd *I Believe in the Resurrection of Jesus Christ* (Hodder, 1975) E.M. B. Green, *Man Alive!* (I.V.P., 1967)
17. Luke 24:39
18. See C. Brown, *History Criticism and Faith: Four Exploratory Studies* (I.V.P., 1976), p. 199
19. Acts 2:36, Acts 4:10. For a discussion of the trustworthiness of the discovery of the empty tomb see W. Pannenberg, *Jesus God and Man* (S.C.M., 1970), p. 101, 104
20. 2 Peter 1:16–21 (T.E.V.)
21. 1 John 1:1–2 (T.E.V.)
22. Psalm 9:10
23. Romans 12:2
24. A. Richardson (ed.) *A Theological Word Book of the Bible* (S.C.M., 1950)
25. *Ibid.*
26. A. S. Peake, *Christianity: Its Nature and Its Truth* (Duckworth, 1907) p. 141
27. *Ibid.*
28. 1 John 4:2